A Guide To Second Date Sex

by Rachel Hirons

Published by Playdead Press 2013

© Rachel Hirons

Rachel Hirons has asserted her rights under the Copyright, Design and Patents Act, 1988, to be identified as the author of this work.

A CIP catalogue record for this book is available from the British Library.

ISBN 978-0-9574491-8-3

Caution

All rights whatsoever in this play are strictly reserved and application for performance should be sought through the author before rehearsals begin. No performance may be given unless a license has been obtained.

This book is sold subject to the condition that it shall not by way of trade or otherwise, be lent, resold, hired out, or otherwise circulated without the publisher's prior consent in any form of binding or cover other than that in which it is published and without a similar condition including this condition being imposed on the subsequent purchaser.

Playdead Press
www.playdeadpress.com

Dirty Stop-Out

Dirty Stop-Out provide exciting and provocative theatre to explore, question and portray the hidden depths of human nature and behaviour through rude, often crude and always voyeuristic comedy. Whether in a bedroom, bathroom or somebody's head, Dirty Stop-Out are masters of making the private public through brutal honesty.

Formed in 2010, Dirty Stop-Out Productions comprises of playwright and screenwriter, Rachel Hirons alongside award winning director, Stef O'Driscoll. Their first play When Women Wee received critical acclaim upon its première performance at the Edinburgh Fringe Festival 2011 before transferring to SOHO Theatre. The film rights were optioned by Damian Jones and the screen play adaptation written by Rachel Hirons entitled Powder Room.

A Guide to Second Date Sex is a co-production between Dirty Stop-Out and TEAfilms. The show premièred at The Edinburgh Fringe Festival, Underbelly, 2012 where it enjoyed a sell-out run and transferred to SOHO Theatre where it enjoyed further sell out success.

TEAfilms

TEAfilms are a London based Film production company with many strands of work headed up by Adam Kes Hipkin and Dan Patrick Hipkin. Their video production repertoire includes; Corporate Videos, Educational Infomercials, Music Videos, Theatre Trailers, Video Design, Films and Documentaries.

Amongst this they have their own line of live music videos in Collaboration with The Fold Studios called TEAfilms Live Sessions. A band or an artist performs one Cover and on Original track in a live recording session.

Recently TEAfilms have shot and co-directed Chronicles of Syntax on the brand new Multiverse channel as well as co-producing A Guide To Second Date Sex, the sell-out phenomenon playing at The Soho Theatre fresh from the Edinburgh Fringe.

A Guide To Second Date Sex was first performed at the Edinburgh Fringe Festival 2012 at The Underbelly. The cast was as follows:

Amy Butterworth	Laura
Thomas O'Connell	Ryan

Written by Rachel Hirons

Directed by Stef O'Driscoll

Video Design by Adam Kes Hipkin & Dan Patrick Hipkin

Produced by Dirty Stop-Out and TEAfilms

Stage Manager Sylvia Darkwa-ohemeng

Company Manager Jennifer Twomey

For my sister... Laura

Character Dialogue
Voice Over
Stage Direction
Film

As the audience enter they are bombarded with projections depicting sex tips and facts regarding sex and relationships. These are shot in a documentary style fashion featuring a male and a female. The videos are projected over the set and the walls with accompanying voice-overs. These include:

FILM #1 A woman's lips offer a subconscious representation of female genitalia. When a woman becomes aroused her genitals become deep red. Wearing red, glossy lipstick is an unconscious attempt to mimic this process and signify a readiness to mate.

FILM #2 Muscles on a man are attractive to women as this not only symbolises agility and strength, essential for a successful hunter gatherer, but ensures the woman that he can provide and protect her and any young.

FILM #3 The majority of a woman's pheromones are released from the top of her head, this is why males often prefer shorter women. This also explains why women stereotypically play with their hair while flirting as to further release the scent.

FILM #4 A woman's flat stomach denotes that she is not yet pregnant. Males prefer females with a flat stomach rather than a bulge, which can imply that another male has beat him to it.

FILM #5 A man's body odour contains valuable information relating to his genes. Women use scent just as much as sight when detecting whether a male will provide her with unhealthy offspring. In support of this theory, research has shown that when confronted with the body odour of a close relation, women often report a 'repulsive' scent.

FILM #6 A males deep voice denotes dominance. A man with a deep voice is likely to be viewed as being of higher status than their squeaky rivals by both sexes, enabling him to potentially achieve more money, more power and ultimately a larger interest from females who appreciate these qualities which assist in the stable upbringing of any potential off spring.

FILM #7 An asymmetrical face is an indication of health problems and genetic abnormalities which occurred even before birth. For this reason symmetrical faces are deemed more attractive by both sexes when choosing a partner.

FILM #8 Men are more attracted to women who carry high levels of oestrogen, the hormone responsible for fertility. There is a direct correlation between blonde hair and high levels of oestrogen, explaining why males are stereotypically believed to find blondes more sexually attractive.

FILM #9 The colour red draws the eye and carries with it powerful, sexual connotations. Research has shown that men rate women who are dressed in the colour red as more attractive than when the same women are not.

FILM #10 Frequently when in the company of someone to which you are attracted, both males and females will unconsciously stand with their hands on their hips with fingers pointed towards their genitalia in order to draw attention to their sexual organs.

FILM #11 Men with lower levels of testosterone experience higher levels nervousness, depression, insomnia, loss of muscle, belly fat, and even smaller anatomy. Men with higher levels of testosterone experience greater self confidence, stronger muscle tissue, more passion for life, and overall healthier lifestyles making them more attractive partners.

FILM #12 Humans use kissing with tongues as a way to ascertain the suitability of a prospective partner. The pheromones that are exchanged in saliva carry details relating to the strength of your immune system and fertility levels. Not only does this enable us to find the most complimentary genetic matches, it also deters us from engaging in reproduction with family members or with people of less ideal genetic matches.

FILM #13 Women rated a good sense of humour as more important than physical attractiveness when asked what they looked for in a partner. Not only does a good sense of humour display a males ability to act competently when faced with a crisis, but stimulates a woman's mind – the largest erogenous zone – more than any visual cue could.

FILM #14 A direct correlation has been found between the length of a males ring finger compared to his index finger of the same hand and high levels of testosterone. The longer the ring finger in comparison, the greater the exposure to testosterone, the higher the sex drive and the more chance of successfully conceiving.

FILM #15 Women are generally attracted to taller males as height not only implies leadership and protective qualities but also exerts dominance over shorter male counterparts allowing taller men a larger selection of potential lovers.

FILM #16 A woman's tendency toward attachment is a biological imperative, a matter of raising offspring successfully. For this reason, when a woman climaxes, she releases a hormone which increases the bond she feels to her partner. This same hormone is also present after child birth to encourage attachment between mother and child.

FILM #17 Men use the condition of a woman's skin as a main indicator into her sex appeal. When shown a single image of a small patch of skin, men were able to correctly determine the level of sexual attractiveness of the female.

As the audience settle, these videos are played at an increasing speed until they over lap, before slowing right down to a final stop.

FILM #18 Depicts RYAN and LAURA in a busy nightclub on the night that they met. Close-ups focus on their features and body language - what they are doing and how - rather than the scenario itself. We see close-ups of her lips and eyes, hands on hips and other stereotypically flirtatious behaviours such as playing with hair, laughing, cleavage on display, high heels, flexing of muscles and pint drinking. We see the couple exchange numbers.

<u>Int. Ryan's Bedroom. 8pm.</u>

There is a bed positioned slightly stage left. To the right of the bed is a toilet, sink and toiletry shelf. A projector screen doubles as a blind behind the bed. It remains down throughout. Down stage right is a pile of DVD's and a TV.

There are clothes piled all over the floor along with dirty dishes and cups. The bed is unmade.

Ryan enters the room, cracks open a beer and drinks before checking his watch.

RYAN: Oh, shit.

In a panic he gulps more beer and turns on Missy Elliot's 'Work It', which he sings along to at times throughout the sequence below.

Ryan frantically begins to gather all of his dirty clothes into one huge pile. He stands holding them, wondering what to do. After a moment he marches out of the room and returns empty-handed. He gathers all of the plates and cups and takes them out of the room. He makes the bed and stares at the now bare room. He ruffles the bed cover and exits. He returns with one dirty plate, one cup and a can of Febreeze. He strategically places the dishes back in his room and sprays the bed with Febreeze. He checks under the bed and pulls two dumbbells out into view.

In the bathroom we watch him gargle mouthwash and gel his hair before turning around with a pair of scissors to trim his pubes into the toilet basin. He re-enters the bedroom, turns off the music and sits on his bed in silence.

RYAN: Should I have a wank? Nah, should probably just leave it. Or maybe I should?

He inserts a hand down the front of his trousers.

Nah you should leave it, just leave it. What time is it?

He checks his phone.

She's late. Might not come. She'll probably come, she said she was.

Pause.

Have I left pubes on the floor in there?

He walks towards the bathroom and checks.

Is that one?

He kicks it with his foot and blows the toilet seat.

Throughout the video sequence below, Ryan is checking over his appearance in his mirror and spraying deodorant.

***FILM #19** We see Laura standing in the street outside a house. She is applying lipstick and checking the rest of her make-up in a mirror. She adjusts her clothes, bends over and ruffles up her hair before standing. She presses the door bell.*

Ryan freezes before composing himself. He exits the bathroom and heads across his bedroom to the door. He does four quick push ups on the floor before before giving in to exhaustion and standing up.

He exits.

Off stage we can hear two people greeting each other and laughing, the conversation is muffled.
This conversation should be improvised by the actors each night.

RYAN (off stage): It's just this one here.

Ryan and Laura enter.

The boudoir.

LAURA: Wow, very nice. Very tidy?

Laura splutters from the deodorant and febreeze that over power the air.

RYAN: Ah, not really. Still got a plate in here from last night. Cup over there.

LAURA: That's all right. What's that, is that a room?

Laura starts walking towards the bathroom.

RYAN: It's a bathroom yeah.

LAURA: Wow, an en suite.

She goes inside the bathroom.

I've always wanted one of these.

Laura begins walking across the room to the en suite.

LAURA
Should I really...? Yes, commit.

RYAN
You just see yourself around then.

Laura begins fluffing her hair and checking inside her nose and teeth.

LAURA
Phew! You do still fancy him then, that's good.

RYAN
Should I sit down?

Ryan sits for a millisecond on the bed before standing up.

Nope stand up, let her lead.

Laura re-enters the bedroom.

LAURA: I've always wanted an en suite. Have you got the biggest room in the house then?

RYAN: Yeah. The *master* bedroom.

Shit! That sounded weird. Like you're a master.

LAURA: Cool. And did you say it was 2 other boys you live with, is it?

RYAN: Yeah, the lads! In our bachelor pad. Ha, on tour...

LAURA: They in?

RYAN: No. Kev's at his mums and Dan's never in.

LAURA: Ah, right.

Don't let there be an awkward silence, not already.

RYAN: Do you wanna drink?

LAURA: Yeah, sure.

RYAN: OK, errm...

Didn't think about this.

I've got Kronenburg, Ribena... milk?

LAURA: *(laughs)* I'll have... whatever.

RYAN: OK, I won't be a sec.

Ryan exits the room.

LAURA
Did he just say milk? Bit weird we're in his room. Should I have shaved? No you won't be shagging tonight. Did he have a razor in that bathroom? I Could use that. Should I sit down? That might be too relaxed. God he is so tall! Much taller than I remember. Is he too tall? No, it's a good thing... I'm gonna sit down. Nope, let him lead. OK, look casual...

Laura repositions herself several times.

Oooh, tell him about that moth the was in that web. That was mad.

Ryan enters and hands her a mug and bottle of pimms.

RYAN: Pimms and... Irn bru.

LAURA: My favourite.

RYAN: Sorry, all the glasses are in, shops.

LAURA: Don't worry.

RYAN: So, how have you been anyway?

LAURA: Good yeah, really good. Oh, I'll tell you what I saw though. I was at the garage down the road, at the cash point, and I saw this huge moth trapped in a spiders web.

RYAN: Shit.

LAURA: And it was flapping like mad and the spider was all over it.

RYAN: Why were you watching this?

LAURA: I was at the cash point and it was there.

RYAN: Oh right.

LAURA: Yeah, and this spider went down and wrapped itself around the wings of the moth to stop it flapping, it was amazing.

RYAN: Did you try and save it?

LAURA: No.

RYAN: Don't get in the way of nature.

LAURA: No I know, that's what I thought.

Pause.

LAURA: I like the little things.

RYAN: Good thing you're with me then.

Laura laughs hysterically at his joke.

RYAN
She is hot.

LAURA: Erm, so what have you been doing?

RYAN: Errr.../

LAURA
That was such a random story. Like, that's what I've been doing.

RYAN: Working mainly.

That sounds shit, something better.

Went round my mates the other night, had some beers, helped him decorate.

That is a lie.

LAURA: Ah, that's nice of you. I suppose you paint the high bits?

RYAN: Ha, yeah.

LAURA: So how tall are you, 6, 4"?

RYAN: 6, 5".

LAURA: Come here, let me stand next to you.

Laura and Ryan walk towards each other. They stand facing at very close proximity.

Wow!

RYAN: While you're down there! Ha.

Laura turns away looking extremely embarrassed. Ryan is also embarrassed.

LAURA: (*Gesturing to the weights on the floor*) Are they yours?

RYAN: Yeah.

LAURA: Are they heavy?

RYAN: Nah, not really. They might be for you though.

LAURA: Can I have a go?

RYAN: Yeah sure, go on.

LAURA: OK!

Laura lifts a weight with one hand. She does a few reps.

LAURA: I can do this, easy.

RYAN: You're not doing it properly though. Here, give it here, I'll show you.

Ryan does 2 reps 'properly'.

RYAN: Like that.

LAURA: How many do you usually do?

RYAN: I usually do about…

50, 200…

100 a day.

LAURA: Wow. Go on then.

FILM #20 Laura's imagination of Ryan looking fit and sweaty easily carrying out the reps.

RYAN: Well like… 1, 2, 3…

Ryan demonstrates until he very quickly tires.

Just like that really.

Ryan quickly puts the weights down.

Right, do you wanna watch a film or something?

LAURA: (*Laughs*) Sure.

RYAN: What you laughing at?

LAURA: I'm not laughing.

RYAN: Cos you think I can't do 100?

LAURA: No/

RYAN: Look I'll show you if you don't believe me.

He goes to pick the weights up again.

LAURA: No I don't want you to show me. I believe you can do 100. Really. Put them down.

Ryan puts them down.

RYAN: Because I can.

LAURA: Ryan, I... I'm very impressed.

I was trying to flirt, never mind.

Right, are we watching a film then or are we going out?

RYAN: Well I thought that we could just chill here, cos I mean, well, we were in a bar last time but, if you wanna go out then.../

LAURA: No that's/

Oh, he definitely thinks we're having sex.

Fine. OK, what film did you have in mind?

RYAN: Err, don't know, whatever you want.

LAURA: Well what have you got?

RYAN: OK, I've got... All the pixar films.

LAURA: Right.

RYAN
Not impressed.

RYAN: OK, I've got Scarface, X-Men, Godfather, trilogy...

LAURA
Here we go.

LAURA: Right I'll look.

Laura walks over to the DVD's.

RYAN
Shit.

Ryan removes a DVD's and hides it behind his back. Laura stares at him.

LAURA: Is that porn?

RYAN: No. Yes. But it's not mine.

LAURA: Sure.

RYAN: No it's not. It's, not mine. It's errm...

Kev, Dan.

Dan's.

LAURA: Why have you got it then?

RYAN: It's errm cos he didn't want his girlfriend to find it.

LAURA: Oh the irony of it, eh?

RYAN: Er, yeah, but you're not my bird yet are ya?

LAURA: Apparently not.

**RYAN
Fuck.**

Long Pause.

RYAN: Awk-waaard.

LAURA: Don't worry.

RYAN: You know what I meant though, like/

LAURA: Yes I know what you meant, it's fine.

RYAN: Err...

LAURA: Yes I know. Right we're watching Cruel Intentions.

RYAN: Ah, good choice.

LAURA
Good choice? Out of what Pixar, porn and Al Pacino?

Ryan begins loading the DVD.

RYAN
Well you fucked that up.

LAURA
Where do we sit? On his bed? This is gonna be awkward.

RYAN
But then again... Cruel Intentions. Pretty sexy stuff.

LAURA
Stay near the edge. Don't get in the bed.

RYAN
You only choose a sexy film, if you want sexy time.

LAURA
OK, just reposition yourself, flat stomach, breathe in. Just lean a bit, too much, yeah like that.

RYAN: Right that's sorted.

Ryan turns around to look at her.

Fuck me that looks uncomfortable.

RYAN: Do you want a top up before it starts?

LAURA: Yes please.

Laura holds out her mug to him.

RYAN
Is that how she usually sits? She looks like a contortionist. Like a sexy contortionist. Yes!

RYAN: Sit up there if you want, then we can see it better.

LAURA: (*cheeky laugh*) Yeah, OK.

They both sit at the top of the bed.

RYAN: Here, get on properly.

Laura and Ryan lie side by side in an awkward manner.

LAURA
Just break this silence.

Long Pause.

LAURA: Have you seen this film before?

RYAN: Yeah, ages ago. This is where that brother and sister get it on?

LAURA: Ha, yeah.

Oh for fucks sake. He blatantly thinks that's why you chose it. You might as *well* have put on the porn.

LAURA: You know this is the film where Ryan Phillipe and Reese Witherspoon met before they got married?

RYAN: No way. Is that his sister in this?

LAURA: No, she's the blonde one that comes in later.

LAURA
The one he *also* has sex with.

RYAN: Is that the actress who was stabbed? Reese errm.../

LAURA: Witherspoon?

RYAN: No, with a knife! Agghaha

Pause. Laura bursts into laughter.

LAURA: You idiot.

RYAN: Sorry.

RYAN
She thinks you're funny.

LAURA
That was so obvious. I look like such an idiot. Say something clever.

LAURA: Oh! Me and my mates won the pub quiz on Wednesday.

RYAN: Wicked.

LAURA: Yeah. Well it was a tie between us and another team so they asked a tie breaker question, what is the real name of the northern lights... and I knew it and the other team didn't.

RYAN: Safe.

Pause.

LAURA: Aurora Borealis.

RYAN: What?

LAURA: The actual name for the northern lights... Aurora Borealis.

RYAN: Oh, cool.

LAURA
I don't know whether you look clever or if that was just weird. Just act cool...

Laura starts playing with her hair in a flirtatious manner.

RYAN
Should I touch her? Or is it too soon?

LAURA
The women in this film are gorgeous... I should have said pixar.

RYAN
Definitely an arm around I think. That's not too much is it? Well she's in your bed, it's going well, I think we can go in for an arm.

LAURA
Is it too late to change the film?

RYAN
Here we go. *(Pause)* Go on. You can do it. Come on, oooh it's happening, it's happening. Boom!

LAURA
Arrrgggghhhh!

RYAN
Smooth. That was smooth.

LAURA
Fuck. OK relax, act calm. What do you do? Do I snuggle in? Maybe I should a bit. Hand on leg? Well that's just asking for it, no hand on leg. We'll snuggle.

Laura snuggles in.

RYAN
Woohoo! And we are snuggling. Do not get a boner. Do not get a boner.

LAURA
Well this makes conversation awkward. We should probably speak.

LAURA: Oh wow, complete works of Austen?

RYAN: Yeah, I don't really...

LAURA: I love her.

RYAN: Yeah? Good.

LAURA: Yeah. Have you read much of her?

RYAN
Say yeah.

RYAN: Yeah.

LAURA: What's your favourite?

RYAN
Errr...

RYAN: All of it really.

LAURA: No preference?

RYAN: Well, there are good bits and bad bits in all of her stuff I think. Which is why I like it all in equal measure. Cos, I mean, some bits start good and then it gets progressively worse and then some ones start shit and then you're like 'this is rubbish' but it gets better towards the end, so it all levels out really.

LAURA: Do you like Emma?

RYAN: Yeah she's all right. Emma, William Shakespeare, all of them.

LAURA: OK.

RYAN: J.K. Rowling, that sort of stuff.

LAURA: Did you read all of the Harry Potters?

RYAN: Didn't need to, I've got the films.

Pause.

RYAN
Phew!

Laura snuggles in further to end the conversation.

Ooh, here we go.

LAURA
That was a total lie. But at least he cared enough to lie. That's kinda sweet, I guess?

RYAN: So what did you get up to the other night when you left the bar?

LAURA: My mate Beth was having some boyfriend issues so I had to make sure she was OK.

RYAN: Did you look after her then?

FILM #21 Laura is sat on a street with her crying friend. Laura is distracted by her phone leaving her friend to cry.

LAURA: Kind of, yeah.

She adjusts her top so that her breasts are more visible.

RYAN
OK, don't get hard, just stay as you are.

Ryan begins stroking Laura's arm.

LAURA
Right. This is happening. This is actually happening, I am going to have sex *with him* tonight. Toilet, razor, gotta be done.

LAURA: Can I use your toilet a sec? Is that all right?

RYAN: Yeah sure, you know where it is?

LAURA: Thanks, I won't be a sec.

RYAN: Should I pause this?

LAURA: No it's fine, I know what happens.

RYAN: Oh all right, safe. See you in a minute.

LAURA: OK.

Laura goes into the bathroom and picks up a razor. She turns around and begins shaving.

LAURA
OK, do this quick, or he'll think you're doing a poo.

RYAN
Well. This is going well. Just... act cool. You're the man. And she is a sexy contortionist.

FILM #22 Depicts Ryan's fantasy of Laura as a sexy contortionist.

LAURA
Well... that's bleeding.

Shit!

It might just stop if you give it a second.

She stands staring at it.

Nope that's not stopping, maybe if I blow on it?

Laura blows on it.

No, should've just left it. I'll sort it out later...
(*Referring to the razor*) **Oo, make sure this is clean first, and...**

She quickly checks in the mirror

We're ready.

Laura exits the bathroom.

LAURA: Hey.

RYAN: Hello again.

LAURA: Did I miss anything good?

RYAN: Errm. Not really.

I did not watch a second of that. Please don't quiz me.

LAURA: Do you want some of this?

RYAN: I've got a beer here, I'm good thanks.

LAURA: More for me.

Laura pours herself some more Pimms.

So, do you usually bring girls into your bedroom on a second date then?

RYAN: Yeah I do actually, there might still be some in here somewhere.

Pause.

No, I'm messing. I er, I don't usually have second dates to be honest.

LAURA: Really? Why?

RYAN: I don't know I just, haven't really found anyone that I like in a while. Dan's been... he keeps trying to set me up on these dates with girls he knows or women he works with and/

LAURA: Oh right, any luck?

FILM #23 Ryan is sat at a dinner table with an older woman who looks exceptionally over sexed – red lipstick, massive cleavage and licking the rim of her glass. CUT TO Ryan in the restaurant toilet on the phone to Dan.

RYAN: 'Dan... she's married... So? Mate I'm not getting involved in some couples weird sex life, no way... No this is the opposite of what I need. She drinks wine by sucking it off her finger...

CUT TO a date where Ryan is sat on a park bench with a girl in tears. Ryan has his arm around her.

RYAN: 'Yeah he does sound like a dick head. You're much better off now. You seem to be doing fine.'

CUT TO his third blind date. Ryan is standing at a bar with his date who is roughly 2 ft smaller than him. Ryan looks annoyed.

RYAN: Yeah. I'm dating all of them, right now.

Laura Laughs.

LAURA: Why do you need Dan's help? You found me easy enough.

RYAN: To be honest I've just not been that interested in... it lately. It was Dan who thought I needed a girlfriend.

LAURA: How come? Is this about an ex or are you just not that into girls?

Please don't be gay.

RYAN: Errmm... I thought you aren't meant to talk about this stuff on dates. Isn't this what they say... That if you talk about it... people, die? I don't know the in's and out's...

LAURA: I think it's fine. It's just getting to know someone isn't it? I don't know why you're not meant to...

Who is she, do you still love her, does she still love you, do you see her?

RYAN: Yeah I suppose, errm, OK yeah, my ex just kinda got with my best mate, my *ex* best mate when I was seeing her and, yeah.

LAURA: WOW. How long ago was that?

Ages, say ages.

RYAN: About ...a year and a bit.

LAURA
Errrm....Yeah, that's ages.

LAURA: And how long where you with her?

RYAN: 2 and a half years. It's all fine now, I mean, we don't hang out or anything but I'm not mad. I say hi if I see either of them...that kinda thing. But yeah, I suppose it put me off.

LAURA: I can see why...

FILM #24 – REMOVED.

RYAN: So what about you?

Laura breaks out of her day dream.

LAURA: You what?

RYAN: You've got to tell me about you after I just told you all that.

LAURA: Errm, OK well, me and my ex broke up... About 8 months ago...

RYAN
Who is he? Do you still love him? Does he still love you? Do you see him?

LAURA
Oh God how do I say he's gay without saying he's gay?

LAURA: And we just became like, mates... like, girly mates.

RYAN: O... K.

Pause.

LAURA: He's gay.

RYAN: OK.

Result! No competition, I'm winning!

RYAN: Did you not see that coming?

FILM #25 Evidence of her ex's homosexuality. Exhibit A him in a facemask, B is homo-erotic art work on his wall, C is Laura holding his hand while he makes flirtatious eye contact with another man in the street.

LAURA: Errm not really... I mean, when I look back now then yes, I can kinda see the signs.

RYAN: Did his boyfriend give him away?

LAURA: No. At the time I just though he had, soft ways. I thought that's how all men are kinda all macho in public and then soft and feminine in private, I thought that was normal.

RYAN: Well yeah that's kinda true but, I mean, you don't usually change your sexuality as well.

LAURA: Yeah I guess.

Pause.

RYAN: So, you turned him gay?

Laura glares at him.

RYAN: I'm joking, I was joking.

Laura play punches Ryan repeatedly.

RYAN: Don't mess with me.

LAURA: You should be fine, you do 100 reps a day.

RYAN: Exactly.

Get her back in the bed.

Are you getting back in bed?

LAURA: No cos you'll tickle me again.

RYAN: I won't. I'm calmly asking you to get in the bed. These are the bedroom rules. Don't break them.

Laura gets in the bed.

LAURA: Is that it then? No other women I have to fight off?

RYAN: I'm kind of a big deal.

Pause.

No. There haven't been many.

LAURA: How many is not many?

RYAN
Really? OK think about this, 6 sounds pathetic, maybe say 30... or 20, is that too low or still too high?

LAURA: Just making up a number?

RYAN: No, I'm trying to remember...

RYAN
16... 18.

18.

LAURA: 18?

RYAN: Why is that a lot?

LAURA: No. But more than not a lot.

RYAN
Too far?

RYAN: OK.

RYAN
Do I ask her?

LAURA
What if he asks?

RYAN
No don't ask her just... please don't be a slag.

Pause.

RYAN: I'm just nippin the loo.

LAURA: OK.

Ryan walks over to the toilet.

LAURA
Shit! Did I just freak him out? Why did I ask that? Don't notice the razor.

RYAN
OK, this is going well... Sex talk, it's looking good. Quick wash. Why didn't I do this earlier?

Ryan begins running the flannel under the tap and washes his genitalia.

In the bedroom Laura is adjusting her boobs in her bra so that they are more 'on display' before straightening out her hair and checking her reflection in a compact mirror. She adjusts her eye make-up and scrambles her possessions back into her bag before taking a huge gulp of her drink and rushing to get back into a casual looking position on the bed.

In the bathroom Ryan is now rigorously drying his penis.

RYAN
Fresh as a daisy.

***FILM #25** Laura's fantasy of Ryan entering the room dressed in tight fitting boxers. The room is lit by candle-light. Ryan looks like a God and she a Goddess. He bites his lip in anticipation of her.*

The video is cut short as Ryan re-enters the bedroom.

RYAN: All right?

LAURA: Hello again. Bedroom rules!

RYAN: Well done, you are learning.

Ryan gets on the bed and puts his arm around Laura.

LAURA
So, do I do the hand on leg?

She puts her hand on his leg.

Too much? Why isn't he touching me back? Shit. Should I take my hand back? Why isn't he touching me?

RYAN
Don't get hard. Do NOT get hard. Should I kiss her? Try and kiss her.

He goes to kiss her as she turns away to get her drink. Too late she turns back to him as he looks away.

Massive fail.

LAURA
Did he just try to kiss you? Shit. This is awful.

RYAN
Maybe just put your head near hers, again.

LAURA
Is he trying again? Do I just kiss him? I'm not kissing him first.

RYAN
Should I try again? Well she didn't want to the first time.

LAURA
I should say something.

RYAN
God she smells good.

LAURA
What should I say?

RYAN
I should tell her.

RYAN: You smell really good.

LAURA: Thanks, so do you.

LAURA
So do you? What the fuck? That's so embarrassing.

At this point Laura's phone begins to ring in her pocket.

RYAN: You're vibrating.

LAURA: Ha, yeah.

Laura looks at her phone and decides not to answer.

RYAN: Go on you can answer, it's fine.

LAURA: No it's probably just/

RYAN: No, go on.

Laura answers her phone, we hear her friend on the other end as a voice-over.

LAURA: Hello?

KATE: Laura there has been a huge fake emergency, you must leave now. Everyone is on fire and dying.

LAURA: Oh yes hi! Yes I'm fine thanks.

KATE: Oh right! Change of plan there is no emergency all the fires are out.

Laura moves herself away from Ryan.

LAURA: Oh that's good to hear, yes sorry I couldn't be there.

KATE: Oooh you dirty bitch. Has he got a big cock?

LAURA: I'm not sure about that at the moment, but I'll look over the stuff and then I'll let you know.

Ryan gestures to leave the room. Laura covers the phone.

LAURA: *(To Ryan)* Oh no, it's OK, I won't be a sec.

RYAN: *(Whispered)* I'll just get another beer.

LAURA: OK.

Ryan exits the room.

LAURA: *(To Kate)* Right he's gone, you are such a bitch.

KATE: Did he hear me?

LAURA: I don't know, I fucking hope not, you sound mental.

KATE: How's it going?

LAURA: Good he's... really nice.

KATE: Nice? Come on give me more than that, I've remembered to call you. What you doing?

LAURA: We're sat in his room.

KATE: You're in his room?

LAURA: Yeah, watching Cruel Intentions.

KATE: Oh you guys are definitely getting it on, who chose that?

LAURA: I did.

KATE: You're filthy.

LAURA: By accident.

KATE: Where are you?

LAURA: Shoreditch. He only lives like, 10 minutes away.

KATE: Convenient.

LAURA: Yeah.

KATE: And what's he like?

LAURA: He's... lovely. I actually like this one he's... really tall, keeps trying to kiss me, quite funny.

KATE: Live with his mum?

LAURA: Nope, not this time.

KATE: Good.

LAURA: 2 lads, Dan and Kevin. But they're not here so...

KATE: Who? He lives with who?

LAURA: Dan and Kevin? I think that's what he said.

KATE: Really tall guy?

LAURA: Yeah.

KATE: Is this Ryan you're talking about?

LAURA: Yeah! Why? How do you know him?

Pause.

Kate?

KATE: Mate that's Big Ryan, that's... Beth's ex.

LAURA: Oh... What?

KATE: That's who Beth was with before she got with Damien. You know when we say 'Big Ryan', well that's him... Big Ryan.

LAURA: Oh fuck, shit, what do...?

KATE: It's fine, calm down.

Ryan re-enters the room.

LAURA: Shit... fucking... Jesus hell!

KATE: Laura...

Laura notices Ryan.

Oh Fuck... errrm... well there's nothing I can do about this right now... I, fucking... just leave it with me... I'll sort it oh, shit it. Just don't say anything and... I'll call you first thing and we'll sort this out, OK?

KATE: Shit son.

LAURA: Right bye.

Laura ends the call looking distressed. Ryan looks very confused.

RYAN: Are... you... OK?

LAURA: Yes. That was work. Everything has just gone, tits up.

Pause.

RYAN: At Pizza Express?

LAURA: Yes.

Pause.

RYAN: What's happened?

Pause.

I thought you were a waitress?

LAURA: Yes, I am.

Pause

It's the tables... they keep moving around the numbers on the tables and... it's just... very confusing.

RYAN: Well, I'm sure you'll get used to it. A change is a good as a rest... as they say.

LAURA: No it's just harder than it looks there's a lot to think about with all the numbers and the.../

Her voice over takes over from her speech.

Laura what the fuck are you talking about just... stop talking...

...Which pizza to give to which person...

Stop Talking, you sound fucking crazy.

...Some don't even want pizza... *(pause)* ...and then there's deserts.

RYAN: Well, maybe just let management know that you want the table numbers to stop changing.

LAURA: Yeah. I'll do that. Good shout.

Ryan gets on the bed.

RYAN: Bedroom rules.

LAURA: Ha! Oh yeah.

Laura sits on the bed. She is stiff and keeps her distance from Ryan who is trying again to watch the film.

RYAN: Has work really got you down?

LAURA: Errm, sorry... No. My mind was just wandering. It was not that.

Do I say something? What do I say? You're my mates ex?

RYAN: You all right there?

LAURA: Yeah, so... I was just thinking about that story you told me about your ex, you must have been really pissed off.

RYAN
This, again?

RYAN: It wasn't the best thing that's ever happened.

LAURA: Do you still talk to her?

RYAN: Nah, haven't got anything to say.

LAURA: Do you hate her?

RYAN: Bit, yeah.

LAURA: If you saw her again would you like, punch her in the face or?

RYAN: No course not.

LAURA: Good, that *is* good.

RYAN: I'd get you to do that.

Pause.

LAURA: Yeah... yeah I'd beat up your ex, but, if she was like you know, a friend or something, then... I couldn't?

RYAN: You couldn't be friends with Beth trust me, she is a bitch.

LAURA: Ah, Beth! Is that her name then?

RYAN: She just hangs around with a bunch of slags.

LAURA: I'm sure they're not all slags.

RYAN: They are.

LAURA: Weeell, you don't know that.

RYAN: I do.

LAURA: How could you know that?

RYAN: Show me your friends and I'll tell you who you are.

LAURA: Not always applicable.

RYAN: Usually is. Like mixes with like.

LAURA: Nope.

RYAN: It's true.

LAURA: You don't even know her friends, and she's not a bitch, she only cheated because the relationship was on it's last legs and you both knew it... Not that I condone cheating but that's what it sounds like to me... from what you've said.

RYAN: Eh?

LAURA: I think you said something like that.

Pause.

Or you implied it.

RYAN: Did I?

LAURA: No. I erm... I know Beth. I met her through a mate like... a year ago and... we're mates. Does that make me a slag?

RYAN
Whhhaaaaatt the fuuuuuck?

RYAN: What the fuck? How did... Did you know that I was... Is that why you're here? Sorry, I don't understand this any more. Hang on a minute... So is this why you're here... Because of Beth?

LAURA: What? No.

RYAN: Why are you here?

LAURA: I didn't even know you were with Beth until I was on the phone.

RYAN: To Pizza Express?

LAURA: No.

Oh God.

It wasn't Pizza Express, it was my friend, and she said it...

RYAN: Who are you?

LAURA: OK, let's just stop.

RYAN: So you lied about being on the phone to work?

LAURA: Well... yes.

RYAN: And all this talk about Beth is because... you knew I went out with her and... what?

LAURA: Because I needed to know if you hated her or still loved her.

RYAN: Why?

LAURA: Because I realised who you were. Big Ryan.

I look mental.

RYAN: What?

LAURA: Do you think I'm mental?

RYAN: Yes.

LAURA: Well, I promise I'm not.

RYAN: Well maybe you're not. But from the evidence, I have to say yes.

LAURA: That's fair.

Pause.

RYAN: So how did your mate know you were on a date with me?

LAURA: She didn't. It was a fake emergency call.

Pause. Ryan looks dazed.

And when I described you, she realised who you were and then told me. That's all.

RYAN: A fake emergency call?

LAURA: Fuck. I didn't mean anything by it. I just, I hardly knew you and... I didn't know about Beth that was...

RYAN: OK.

LAURA: I'm sorry. I've fucked this haven't I?

Pause in which Ryan softens to Laura who is showing genuine remorse.

LAURA: *(awkwardly)* Would you like me to leave?

RYAN: Do you want to leave?

LAURA: Well... I don't know. Can we move on from this?

RYAN: To be honest... Actually, yes. I can move on. Quite happily. I have moved on, a long time ago. Can you?

LAURA: Yes. Fine. Good. (*Pause*) Sorry about that.

RYAN: No that's fine.

Women are fucking crazy.

RYAN: So they didn't move the table numbers around?

LAURA: No.

RYAN: Thank God for that.

LAURA: But once they did do that once.

Laura snuggles into Ryan again. They make eye contact.

RYAN
Right I'm going in.

They kiss passionately and begin intertwining their legs. Ryan puts his hand on Laura's face.

RYAN
Start with the face and work your way down.

Laura begins stroking down Ryan's chest.

RYAN
OK this is happening. Don't get over excited. Just stay calm. I am not calm.

LAURA
Am I being too forward? Is this too much?

Ryan puts his hand on Laura's breast.

LAURA
Oh my God.

RYAN
Oh my God.

LAURA
Take control. Take control.

Laura straddles him.

RYAN
I should've had a wank.

Laura starts lifting his shirt.

RYAN
Wow.

LAURA
Where am I going with this?

RYAN
She is so confident. How many guys has she had?

LAURA
Right I'll start with his shirt, kiss for a bit and then I'll take off mine and that is the new plan.

RYAN
You're gonna have to be good at this. All your best moves.

Laura starts unbuttoning her shirt.

You can't let her take off her own shirt.

Ryan tries to manoeuvre it so he is in control but it just breaks up the sequence.

Laura starts removing her shoes. Ryan starts un-belting his trousers. Laura notices this and so starts taking off her own trousers.

LAURA
This is the most awkward situation that has ever happened.

RYAN
This, is great.

Laura lets out an awkward laugh. Eventually Laura is in her underwear. Ryan is wearing unbuttoned jeans.

LAURA
I need to turn off the light. I can't just walk over there.

LAURA: Erm, can we turn off the light?

RYAN: It's a bit bright that light isn't it?

LAURA: Yeah just a bit.

Ryan walks across the room and turns off the light. In the darkness he removes his trousers.

LAURA: Do you have a lamp?

RYAN: Erm yeah.

Ryan turns the lamp on which shines on the bed. He quickly grabs his crotch.

RYAN: Is that OK?

LAURA: Perfect.

RYAN: Not too dark?

LAURA: Not at all.

Ryan gets back into bed.

LAURA: Breathe in, Boobs out.

Laura and Ryan begin kissing and snuggling. Laura disappears under the cover.

RYAN
Yes! OK relax... oh wow... this is... I can't wait to tell Dan about this... Who's the daddy now, Dan? Gotta tell him about that porno as well, in case she asks him... right just stop thinking... stop thinking... This is a result... don't get too carried away now... I hope it's all clean down there... what if it's too clean... can she taste soap? Can she breathe under there? Should I lift the cover? Give her some air? A little air hole? *(Ryan 'wafts' the cover slightly)* OK... God she's good...

LAURA
I can't breathe... should I stop yet? I don't know how long I should do this for... Maybe a few more swirly ones then I'll stop... They always work like a charm.

Laura comes up from under the covers.

RYAN: Thank you.

They start kissing and Ryan goes on top.

RYAN
Am I meant to go down there?

LAURA
Oh please don't go down there.

RYAN
Is that what she's expecting?

LAURA
Don't do it, don't do it.

Ryan starts shimmying down the bed and under the covers.

LAURA
Nooooo.

RYAN
Oh god, where is it?

Pause.

LAURA
What's he doing?

RYAN
I can't see shit. Oh, it's here.

LAURA
OK. Here we go. OK, relax. He seems fine. This is good.

RYAN
Who the fuck designed this? Oo, where's it gone?

LAURA
Wow, he is good.

RYAN
(slowly)
B, C, D, E, F, G... G is a hard one.

LAURA: Ryan, do you have any, erm... condoms?

Ryan re-emerges.

RYAN: Yeah... there's some just under here, I'll grab one. *Ryan runs his hand underneath the side of the mattress and then along the entire rim of the mattress while Laura does her best to cover herself up.*

Ryan: They were just here, I swear they were, hang on...Oh I can feel something.... Here! Here they are. Right erm, what do you want, I've got Banana or it might just be yellow, one that makes everything burn.

LAURA: Not that one.

RYAN: No I don't like them either, errm, ribbed or glow in the dark, I'd prefer if my cock doesn't glow to be honest.

LAURA: Banana.

RYAN: Ma' lady would like banana...

LAURA: Here, I'll do it.

RYAN: I think I've got it the right way round.

Laura attempts to fit the condom on Ryan with her mouth, this takes a few seconds.

LAURA: No, it is just yellow.

RYAN: Oh is it?

Ryan takes the lead and positions Laura on the bed, him on top. He begins fumbling around.

LAURA: No not there, it's just... it's higher, HIGHER!

RYAN: Oh shit, sorry.

LAURA: Here give it to me.

RYAN
Woohoo and we're off. Hard as you can, come on!

FILM #25 The projector shows a montage of sex scenes reminiscent of sex for approximately 1 minute.

FILM #26 The projector begins showing Laura and Ryan as they are having sex right now.

LAURA
I feel like we've been doing this for ages. Is he ever gonna come? He doesn't fancy me... Oh God what if he doesn't fancy me... Am I not moving enough? OK, squeeze harder... harder... I must have a massive vagina!

RYAN
OK, Don't come, don't come, look at something else focus on the pillow.

LAURA
Is he even looking at me? I bet he's thinking of someone else.

RYAN
Think of something else... something else... ermmm.

FILM #27 Flashing on the screen along with the video of Ryan and Laura having sex are images of maths equations and the alphabet backwards on Ryan's forehead.

RYAN
....I'm gonna come... Arrgghhh, oh, fuck oh fuck... Has she noticed? I don't think she's noticed. Maybe I can just carry on. Yeah that should be fine.

LAURA
Did he just come? I'm pretty sure he did. Do I just let him carry on? I can't do that. What do I say? Maybe just smile at him as if to say 'I know'?

Pause.

RYAN
Why is she smiling like that? She's loving it, she is absolutely loving it. Got away with THAT one.

LAURA: Ryan, erm, did you...? Have you... finished?

RYAN: Errm...

Do I lie? Oh she's gonna know.

RYAN: Yes, I did, but I can carry on it's fine.

LAURA: No it's OK you can stop, we can stop. Ryan, stop.

Ryan gets off and lies next to Laura.

RYAN
I did really shit – maybe I should apologise?

RYAN: Sorry about that.

LAURA: About what?

RYAN: Well, y'know? I'll do better next time.

LAURA
There's gonna be a next time?

Pause.

RYAN
Yes. There's gonna be a next time.

Laura kisses Ryan's arm and snuggles in. They comfortably begin watching the television.

LAURA
I need a wee.

RYAN
I'm still wearing this bloody condom.

LAURA: We're not really watching this film are we?

RYAN: What? I've been watching the whole thing. I'm only joking.

Laura laughs. Ryan begins fumbling under the cover.

LAURA: Are you still in the condom?

RYAN: Yeah.

LAURA: *(In the tone of Ryan)* Allow me.

Laura gets it off him and throws it on the floor.

LAURA: Oh, do you have a bin?

RYAN: You've already thrown it on the floor so, what does it matter?

Laura and Ryan snuggle down together and look relaxed and comfortable.

LAURA: Do you really do 100 reps a day?

RYAN: No.

Big pause.

LAURA: I may have used your razor.

RYAN: I know you did.

We hear a few lines from the film Cruel Intentions. Ryan and Laura snuggle and share a kiss. Ryan leans across to turn off the lamp.

FILM #28 'To be continued...'

The lights fade to black.